TRANSGENDER PIONEERS

CAITLYN JENNER

Carla Mooney

ROSEN
PUBLISHING

New York

Published in 2017 by The Rosen Publishing Group, Inc.
29 East 21st Street, New York, NY 10010

Copyright © 2017 by The Rosen Publishing Group, Inc.

First Edition

Library of Congress Cataloging-in-Publication Data

Names: Mooney, Carla, 1970- author.
Title: Caitlyn Jenner / Carla Mooney.
Description: New York : Rosen Publishing, 2017. | Series: Transgender
. pioneers | Audience: Grades 7-12. | Includes bibliographical references
and index.
Identifiers: LCCN 2015048642 | ISBN 9781508171584 (library bound)
Subjects: LCSH: Jenner, Caitlyn, 1949- | Transgender people--United
States--Biography--Juvenile literature. | Transgender athletes--United
States--Biography--Juvenile literature. | Track and field athletes--United
States--Biography--Juvenile literature.
Classification: LCC HQ77.8.J46 M66 2016 | DDC 306.76/8092--dc23
LC record available at http://lccn.loc.gov/2015048642

Manufactured in China

CONTENTS

INTRODUCTION

Caitlyn Jenner appears at the 2015 Glamour Women of the Year Awards on November 9, 2015.

On April 24, 2015, nearly 17 million people turned on their televisions to watch Caitlyn Jenner (then known as Bruce Jenner, the name she was given by her parents at birth) sit down for an interview with ABC News journalist Diane Sawyer. For months, rumors had swirled around the Olympic champion and reality television star. Her appearance had changed over the previous few years, with noticeable plastic surgery to her face and a tracheal shave. She had grown her hair longer and had been spotted wearing earrings and nail polish. In recent months, the paparazzi storm surrounding her had intensified. Questions abounded: Was she a gay man? Was she a cross-dresser? Was she transgender? Photographers followed her every move. She endured the whispers, innuendos, and talk show jokes in silence. But on April 24, it was finally her turn to speak.

With cameras set up inside Jenner's Malibu home, the interview opened with an emotional Jenner welcoming Sawyer. Obviously uncomfortable and admittedly apprehensive, Jenner was quiet at first. She paused and then explained that she had been thinking about this moment for most of her life. Jenner told Sawyer that she had been confused about her gender identity since she was a young child. She explained that her brain and soul were much more female than male. And, for the first time in her sixty-five-year life, she revealed publicly that although she had been assigned a male gender at birth, she was, in fact, a woman.

Jenner's revelation that she was a transgender woman resonated around the world. Many transgender people watching that night were apprehensive, unsure of how someone with so much celebrity would portray and reflect their community. Some, including Drian Juarez, manager of the Los Angeles LGBT Center's Transgender Economic Empowerment Project, were pleasantly surprised that the interview sensitively discussed gender pronouns and described in detail what it means to be transgender. Juarez and others praised the interview for discussing serious issues faced by transgender people, such as violence and poverty.

Jenner, because of her celebrity as an athlete and a reality television star, was now in a unique and powerful position. Going public with her transition, she had the ability to reach millions of people—spanning several generations—through social media. Jenner's story became part of an expanding movement to raise awareness of transgender issues. Jenner helped put a highly visible face to the story, thereby improving visibility for other members of the transgender community.

While the public may mark the *20/20* interview as the beginning of Caitlyn Jenner's story, for Jenner, that story had begun sixty-five years earlier.

CHAPTER 1

ALL-AMERICAN ATHLETE

On October 28, 1949 in Mount Kisco, New York, William Jenner and his wife, Esther, welcomed their second child into the world. At the time, William, a tree surgeon, and Estelle, a housewife, named their child William Bruce Jenner. Jenner was assigned a male gender at birth. Today, we know Jenner by her chosen name, Caitlyn Marie.

From a very young age, Caitlyn showed that she had inherited the family's athletic talent. In 1945, her father, William, had competed in the U.S. Army Olympics in Nuremburg, Germany, winning a silver medal in the 100-yard dash. Her grandfather had also competed in sports, running the Boston Marathon several times. By the time Jenner was two years old,

Caitlyn Jenner grew up in scenic Mount Kisco, New York.

her physical build and endless energy already hinted that she might one day follow her father and grandfather into sports. As a toddler, she was so active that her parents nicknamed her "Bruiser." They even had to put up a fence around their yard to keep her from bolting

LET'S TALK ABOUT GENDER PRONOUNS

When discussing members of the transgender community, it is important to be sensitive about how a trans individual chooses to be referred to. For instance, although many transgender individuals use pronouns that correspond to their assigned gender (the gender that their parents and their doctor assigned them at birth—generally based on anatomical features) throughout their youth and up until they come out as trans, it is considered respectful to refer to them with their chosen pronouns—even when discussing their life before transitioning. Therefore, we refer to Caitlyn by her chosen name and with female pronouns ("she," "her," and "herself"), even when discussing her childhood and adult life prior to transition.

When in doubt, always ask a transgender person which pronouns they prefer. If you cannot ask, use gender-neutral pronouns (such as "they," "them," and "themself") or pronouns consistent with their appearance and gender expression.

off. When she still managed to find ways out, William and Estelle resorted to tethering Caitlyn to a clothesline anchored in the middle of the lawn to avoid her running off.

CHALLENGES AT SCHOOL

While running and jumping came easily to young Caitlyn, schoolwork was more challenging. She struggled with reading and dreaded each time a teacher would choose her to read in front of the class. By the time Caitlyn was in second grade, she still could not read. Teachers believed that Caitlyn was either lazy or unintelligent, and the school decided to make her repeat the grade.

At home, Caitlyn's older sister Pam and her mother noticed some puzzling signs. One day, Pam saw that Caitlyn had arranged the family's set of encyclopedia books oddly. Instead of ordering the volumes from A to Z moving left to right, Caitlyn had placed them moving from right to left. In addition, Pam noticed that Caitlyn frequently spelled words backward, for one, the word "saw" as "was." When helping Caitlyn with her spelling list, Esther Jenner noticed that Caitlyn could spell the words correctly one day, but then get them wrong the next. She scolded

Caitlyn for not concentrating and urged her to focus more.

Caitlyn's struggles in school continued through junior high. Then, a school doctor finally put a name to her problems and diagnosed Caitlyn with dyslexia. Dyslexia is a learning disability that causes a person to have difficulty processing language, reading, and spelling. Even knowing the diagnosis, Caitlyn's school was not well equipped to handle the learning disorder. Jenner remembers that after telling her, the school doctor simply sent her back to class.

Dealing with dyslexia was a challenge for Caitlyn. She struggled with poor self-esteem and felt that everyone else at school was so much better than she was. In an interview published in the August/September 1999 issue of *ABILITY Magazine*, Jenner described how it felt. She shared, "The biggest problem with dyslexic kids is not the perceptual problem, it is their perception of themselves. That was my biggest problem. I thought everybody else was doing much better than I was. I'd look around to my peers, and everyone else could do this simple process of reading, but for me it wasn't working. If you are a kid, reading is really important stuff." Still, Jenner says that her dyslexia and the insecurities it created forced her to work hard and gave her the determination to succeed.

SECRETS AT HOME

At the same time she was struggling at school, Caitlyn was also dealing with secrets at home. Around the age of eight or nine, Caitlyn found herself fascinated by her mother's and sister's clothing. Sometimes, she would sneak into their rooms to try on a dress and wrap a scarf around her head. At the time, Caitlyn did not have a name for the feelings she was having.

In the late 1950s, very few people had heard of being transgender. (In fact, the term transgender itself wasn't coined until 1965 by a psychiatrist. Prior to that, transgender individuals were referred to as "transsexual.") In 1952, Christine Jorgensen, a World War II veteran who had been assigned male at birth traveled to Denmark for sex reassignment surgery (SRS), a doctor-supervised surgical intervention that some transgender people choose to undergo as part of their transition. Such a procedure was not yet available in the United States. Jorgensen's story became

Christine Jorgensen is photographed in her London hotel room on August 6, 1954.

public in December 1952 when the *New York Daily News* published an article about her, including portions of a letter she had written to her parents saying that nature had made a mistake that she had corrected. When she returned to the United States in 1953, Jorgensen was met by reporters. Many members of the public and the media ridiculed her decision. Even the U.S. government did not recognize her as a woman, and she was denied a marriage license in 1959 because her birth certificate still listed her as a man.

Without awareness of the transgender community, Caitlyn kept her thoughts and feelings to herself. She experimented with women's clothing in secret, scared for anyone to find out. She marked the closet so that she could put the clothing back in exactly the same place and nobody would know she had been there. Jenner says that at the time, she did not know why she wanted to wear women's clothes. She just knew that it made her feel good.

FINDING SUCCESS AND FITTING IN

In fifth grade, a new world opened up for Caitlyn, one that would change her life. One day at school, a gym teacher lined up chairs and had each student run laps around them while being timed. To her own surprise as well as the surprise of her classmates and teachers, Caitlyn clocked in as the fastest runner in the school. Jenner says that it was the first time that she really accomplished anything at school. Suddenly the praise that had eluded Jenner in the classroom was being given to her because of her athletic talent. She enjoyed the attention and realized that sports might be her path to success. "So all of a sudden sports became very intriguing to me. It became important especially later on when I was a little older. I would show up on the football field and challenge a guy who was a good student, good reader, and BOOM! I'd clean his clock! I said, boy, I like this, this is fun! I could do it better than most of the other kids in school. So for me sports became my little niche in life," she recalled in her 1999 interview with *ABILITY Magazine*.

In high school, Caitlyn became a talented and popular athlete, first at Sleepy Hollow High School in Westchester County, New York, and later at Newtown High in Sandy Hook, Connecticut, after her family moved. She excelled at basketball, football, and track, earning several most valuable player awards. In the summers, Caitlyn took to the water and became a champion water skier, winning the Eastern States water-skiing championship three times.

Although she was enjoying success in sports, Caitlyn still continued to struggle with her gender identity. She says that she would look at the men and women around her, noticing how comfortable they appeared to be with themselves. "I look at guys and I go, 'He's comfortable in his own skin,'" Jenner explained in an April 2015 interview with ABC News. "And I thought, 'Wouldn't that be a nice way to go through life?' I look at women all the time thinking, 'Oh my God, how lucky are they that they can wake up in the morning and be themselves.' But me, I'm stuck here in the middle."

A NEW DIRECTION: THE DECATHLON

In 1968, Jenner attended Graceland College in Lamoni, Iowa, on a football scholarship. After a knee injury sidelined Jenner during her freshman year, one of the track coaches suggested that Jenner try the decathlon. The decathlon is one of track's premier and most grueling events. Athletes compete over two days in ten track and field events, including the long jump, high jump, sprinting, hurdles, discus, and javelin. The event is such a test of athletic skill that the Olympic gold medal winner is often called the world's greatest athlete.

Under the coaching of L.D. Weldon, Jenner jumped into the new challenge. On her first attempt at the decathlon in 1970, she broke the school record. After that, Jenner embraced this new athletic direction and began to seriously train for the event. Her training quickly paid off, and in April 1971, Jenner won the decathlon at the Kansas Relays, a three-day track meet held at the University of Kansas that attracts track and field athletes from around the country. She also became a small college "all-American," an honor given to outstanding collegiate athletes.

In 1972, Jenner qualified to compete in the Olympic trials in Eugene, Oregon. At the trials, thirty decathlon athletes would compete for three spots on the U.S. Olympic team. Few expected Jenner, a relative newcomer to the sport, to make the team. At the end of the first day of the trials, Jenner was in eleventh place. On the second day, she steadily advanced with each event. By the end of the day, she reached third place and had earned a spot on the Olympic team. It was the biggest athletic thrill of her life.

The Kansas Relays at the University of Kansas has been one of the most popular track-and-field events in the United States since they began in 1923. Photographed here is the 2005 relays.

The Olympiapark in Munich, Germany, where the 1972 Summer Olympics were held.

In August, Jenner traveled to Munich, Germany, for the 1972 Summer Olympics. There, she flashed glimpses of future greatness and finished tenth in the world. Jenner says that she remembers looking at the decathlon winner with envy as the victor stood on the podium and received the gold medal. On the plane ride home to Iowa, Jenner vowed that she would return to the next Olympics and win the gold.

CHAPTER 2

TRAINING TO BE THE BEST

Back in the United States, Jenner threw herself wholeheartedly into training. One of her biggest supporters was her first wife, Chrystie Crownover. Crownover, the daughter of a minister from southeastern Washington State, met Jenner while at Graceland College in 1968. Although they did not hit it off at first, the pair eventually got together. By Jenner's senior year, they were seriously dating.

From the start, Crownover helped to take care of everything Jenner needed. She tutored Jenner, so well in fact that Jenner made dean's list in her senior year. After Jenner's tenth-place finish at the Munich Olympics, Crownover vowed that she would do everything she could to help Jenner

Chrystie Crownover (left) and Caitlyn Jenner (right) pose together at a tennis match in New York City in 1977.

win the gold. Three months after Jenner returned from Munich, she and Crownover married.

While Jenner was deep in training, it fell upon Chrystie to support the couple financially. She dropped out of college and took a job as a flight attendant. Jenner worked part-time selling life insurance, but it was Chrystie's salary that kept the couple afloat. Her job with United Air came with a valuable perk: free tickets for herself and Jenner that allowed the couple to travel together to decathlon events around the world. In addition, Chrystie shouldered most of the responsibilities at home. She managed the checkbook, cooked meals, and kept Jenner focused on training.

TRAINING IN CALIFORNIA

In the 1970s, California was a major training center for Olympic track and field athletes. Although Los Angeles was the main track center of the state, San Jose was building its reputation as a track training town. Many athletes trained under the supervision of Team USA coaches at San Jose Community College.

Jenner knew that she could not go any further in Iowa. If she wanted to compete for a gold medal, she needed to seriously train year-round with the country's best athletes. So Jenner and Chrystie moved to San Jose in 1973. The apartment they rented was tiny, but it was right next to a track.

In San Jose, Jenner trained every day for six to eight hours. She trained with the best track and field athletes in the United States, including Al Feuerbach, the current world record holder in shot put; Mac Wilkins and John Powell, 1976 Olympic medalists in discus; Olympic gold medal–winning sprinter Millard Hampton; and hurdler Andre Phillips. "If you train with

Mac Wilkins, who trained with Jenner in San Jose in the early 1970s, participates in the discus throw at the TAC (now known as USA Track & Field) Championships on October 1, 1988.

a decathlon man," Jenner told the New York Times in 1976, "you can't visualize that you can do much better. But if you throw the discus with Mac Wilkins or throw the shot with Al Feuerbach, then they're 20 feet ahead of me. You learn much more that way."

The intense training paid off on the track. Over the next few years, Jenner won the Amateur Athletic Union decathlon title in 1974 and 1976 and the 1975 Pan American Games. She was also ranked number one in the world in the decathlon and held the world-record of 8,524 points.

All the while, Chrystie supported her partner's quest for the gold. When Jenner hit a slump, Chrystie kept her focused. "She gave me a hard time until 3 AM, about giving 100 percent," Jenner said in a May 1976 article in People. "She said, 'I'll take care of the finance, you just run!' One month later, I had the world record."

KEEPING SECRETS

In the early days of their marriage, Chrystie noticed a rubber band attached to one of her bras. She asked Jenner about it. At first, Jenner pretended that she knew nothing about it. Later, she confessed to Chrystie that she had been wearing her clothes and had used the rubber band to stretch the bra around her wider frame. Jenner revealed that she had always identified as a woman. It was the first time Jenner had told anyone about her feelings.

At first, Chrystie was shocked by Jenner's revelation. "I can't remember the exact words because it was such a shock to me," Chrystie said in an April 2015 interview on *Good Morning America.* "…He told me he always wanted to be a woman, and understandably I was speechless. It was so hard to wrap your head around it, particularly because he was such a manly man." (At the time, Chrystie still referred to Caitlyn with masculine pronouns.) At the same time, Chrystie says that she felt extremely grateful that Jenner was sharing something so personal with her. "If he had been wanting to dress up when he was with me or any of those things it would have been different. But he was still masculine. He was still my hero. He was still pursuing this goal of being the greatest athlete in the world. It wasn't like it was a hard thing to handle. It was like a piece of information he shared with me and then he went back to being a real guy," she said in an article in *Vanity Fair* in July 2015.

Internally, Jenner struggled with her gender identity—a struggle that can lead to depression and confusion, known as gender

TRANSGENDER PIONEER: RENÉE RICHARDS

Long before transgender rights became the subject of vast cultural attention, Renée Richards was a pioneer in the transgender community. An eye surgeon and professional tennis player, Richards transitioned in the 1970s. A year after Richards's sex reassignment surgery in 1975, the United States Tennis Association (USTA) banned her from the 1976 U.S. Open. Richards filed a lawsuit against the USTA to fight the ban. She argued that being able to play in the tournament indicated acceptance of her right to be a woman. In 1977, the New York State Supreme Court ruled in Richards's favor, making a landmark decision for transgender rights. The judge ruled that the USTA had intentionally discriminated against Richards. The judge also granted an injunction against the USTA, which allowed her to play in the U.S. Open. Through her fight to play tennis as a woman, Richards became a role model and spokesperson for the transgender community. In 2000, the USTA inducted Richards into its hall of fame.

Renée Richards preceded Caitlyn Jenner as a beloved American athlete who came out as trans.

dysphoria. Instead of dealing with it, she pushed the feelings aside and focused on the goal ahead of her: the 1976 Olympics.

1976 OLYMPIC DECATHLON

In July 1976, the Jenners arrived in Montreal for the Olympics. The decathlon had long been dominated by American athletes. Beginning with Jim Thorpe in 1912, an American had won the event in every Olympics from 1912 to 1968, except for three. In 1972, Soviet athletes Mykola Avilov and Leonid Lytvynenko won the gold and silver medals. In the 1970s, tensions were high between the United States and the Soviet Union. In Montreal, Jenner's main rival was the defending Soviet decathlon champion, Avilov. Americans rallied behind Jenner, an all-American athlete competing for the country.

On the first day of competition, Jenner broke her personal best in the 100-meter dash. Then she achieved personal bests in the next four events—long jump, shot put, high jump, and the 400-meter sprint. Avilov beat Jenner in three of the first-day events and achieved personal bests of his own in three events. Yet it did not matter. By the end of the first day, Jenner was just 35 points behind the leader. She had run faster, thrown farther, and jumped better than she ever had in her athletic career. And she still had all of her best events ahead of her on day two. Jenner says that after the 400-meter sprint, she knew that she was on her way to winning the gold.

On the second day of the decathlon, Jenner crushed the competition in the final five events. She tossed the discus for an average of more than fifty meters, nearly three meters farther than the next competitor. When she cleared 15-9 on the pole vault, Jenner took the overall lead. After a good javelin throw, she knew that she would be able to beat Avilov's world record decathlon score. In the final event, the grueling 1,500-meter run, Jenner knew that she only needed an average time to win the gold medal. She started slowly, preserving energy for the end of the race. Yet as the crowd cheered her on, she ran faster and faster, finishing in second place behind the fastest athlete in the competition. She crossed the finish line an Olympic champion.

After Jenner finished the 1,500-meter run, a fan raced onto the track and handed her a United States flag on a stick. Jenner grabbed the flag and waved it as she jogged a victory lap around the track. In that moment, she created one of the most iconic moments in sports history, which

Jenner finishes first in the 1,500-meter dash at the 1976 Summer Olympics.

has been repeated by American athletes after victories ever since. Spotting a tearful Chrystie at the railing, Jenner ran over and pulled her onto the track. The couple embraced. Together, they had achieved a goal set four years earlier in Munich—that Jenner would win the Olympic gold medal.

WORLD'S GREATEST ATHLETE

Not only had Jenner won the Olympic gold medal, she had shattered Avilov's world record, scoring 8,618 total points. With her dominant performance over the two-day competition, she had become the world's greatest athlete. "It takes a decathlon athlete to truly appreciate what Jenner has done," said 1968 decathlon gold medalist Bill Toomey in an August 1976 *Time* magazine article. "It was total artistry, a beautiful composition."

At the medal ceremony, Jenner stood on the highest of three platforms, with silver medalist Kratschmer on her right and bronze medalist Avilov on her left. She bent down to receive the long-coveted gold medal around her neck. Heavy and shiny, the medal was the crown jewel in her athletic accomplishments. And it would also be her last. Jenner had announced before the Montreal Games that this would be her last meet. "When I walked off the field after the medal ceremony, I glanced around one more time and then walked away. That was the end of the decathlon for me. I never even went back and got my vaulting poles. I left them there in the stadium. They're a hassle to travel with and I was finished with them," she said in *Decathlon Challenge*, an autobiography she published in in 1977.

While she celebrated the greatest achievement of her career, Jenner still was not at peace with herself. The night of her Olympic victory, she and Chrystie stayed in a Montreal hotel. The following day, she stood in front of a mirror wearing nothing but the gold medal around her neck. Even though she was considered to have the world at her fingertips, Jenner once again felt confused and insecure. Instead of seeing a champion, she saw the dyslexic kid who used to struggle to read in front of her classmates. She felt as if she had been living a lie and trying to fake out the rest of the world. Now that the challenge of the decathlon was over, she wondered what she would do next.

CHAPTER 3

LIVING WITH FAME

Winning the decathlon gold medal made Jenner an American hero. Tens of millions of Americans had watched her on television and cheered as she ran a victory lap carrying the American flag. Jenner's victory became a source of great pride for Americans. The year Jenner won was the country's bicentennial—or two-hundredth birthday—and the year was filled with patriotic events and celebrations. In 1976, Jenner received two additional honors, being named the Associated Press Athlete of the Year and receiving the Sullivan Award for the best amateur athlete in the United States.

Even before the Montreal Olympics, Jenner knew that winning the gold would be her ticket to the future. She planned to use her victory to open the door for new opportunities. In the 1970s, Olympic athletes had amateur status. Unlike professional athletes, amateur athletes were not allowed to receive payment for their celebrity. In order to profit from her fame, Jenner would have to give up her amateur status, disqualifying her from any future Olympic competition.

RETURNING A HERO

A few days after winning the gold, Jenner and Chrystie returned to the United States. They stopped at her parents' house, where a crowd of people waited to celebrate with the couple. Next, they flew into New York City, where strangers congratulated them everywhere they went. When walking down the street, people yelled from cars and across the street. One man even stopped his car in the middle of traffic and jumped in the street, shouting and waving his hands above his head.

While in New York, the Jenners' new public relations firm organized a press conference. Sixty media outlets arrived, along with cameramen from major television stations and reporters from many radio stations. That afternoon, photographs of the Jenners appeared in New York newspapers. At dinner at a popular New York restaurant, the congratulations continued to

Jenner's gold medal at the 1976 Summer Olympics instantly made her an American celebrity.

pour in, with the couple turning down bottles of champagne sent to their table by fellow diners.

Overnight, Jenner had become a household name. Millions of Americans had watched on television sets in their living rooms as Jenner jumped, vaulted, and ran into their hearts. She was charming, good looking, and seemed grateful for her success, without being boastful or putting on airs. She had become an old-fashioned American hero. Chrystie had also become a celebrity in her own right through the ABC network's television coverage of the Olympics as well as features and interviews on other television networks and with national magazines.

INSTANT CELEBRITY

The demand for Jenner was almost instantaneous. George Wallach, the head of a Beverly Hills firm that specialized in radio and TV time sales, was a personal friend of the Jenners and became their personal manager on July 31, 1976. The day after Jenner's victory, a men's toiletry company offered $50,000 for a single one-minute commercial. Wallach turned the offer down. He had bigger things in mind for the Jenners.

After a brief Hawaiian vacation with Chrystie, Jenner threw herself into capitalizing on her Olympic fame. In the ten weeks after winning

Jenner appears with friend and fellow Olympian gold medalist Rafer Johnson in 1972.

the gold medal, she appeared as a guest on four national television interview or variety shows. She was featured on the cover of the August 9, 1976, issue of *Sports Illustrated* magazine. She also teamed with Rafer Johnson to play in a celebrity doubles tennis match on national television. She spent four days with her father in a Louisiana swamp, working with an alligator relocation crew for an episode of the television show *The American Sportsman*. In addition, she attended a state dinner at the White House, seated next to first lady Betty Ford. Jenner was even selected in the seventh round of the 1976 National Basketball Association draft by the Kansas City Kings, although she never played for them.

Good-looking, young, and charming, Jenner proved to be irresistible to the American public. Within four months of returning from Montreal, she signed a two-year sports broadcasting contract with ABC, which was later expanded to four years. Her appearances on television occurred at the same time that television viewership greatly increased, with ESPN and other cable channels emerging. In this era, athletes like Jenner were able to find more opportunities on camera and in the media. On camera, Jenner shone. She seemed like an all-American hero, full of vitality and cheer.

Over the next four years, Jenner worked almost non-stop. In 1976, producers of the upcoming Superman film thought that Jenner might be the perfect fit for the film's leading role. They flew her to Rome to screen test for the part. However, Jenner was eventually passed over when producers decided she looked too young on screen for the role, and the part was eventually given to actor Christopher Reeve.

In 1977, Jenner appeared on the cover of boxes of Wheaties breakfast cereal and became a spokesperson for the Wheaties brand. When the San Francisco district attorney sued Wheaties for false advertising, Jenner held a press conference and insisted that she ate Wheaties several times a week and the cereal was an important part of her training diet.

Riding her Olympic success, she promoted several products, including Norelco shavers, Minolta cameras, bikes, and weight-lifting equipment. There was a Jenner clothing line and Jenner sneakers. Jenner was one of the first athletes to turn success on the field into financial opportunities elsewhere. In a December 2002 article in *Sports Illustrated*, Jenner joked, "Nobody's worked one performance better than I have. I was in that stadium 48 hours and now you can't get rid of me."

Jenner also co-authored a book, *Decathlon Challenge*, the story of her journey to Olympic gold. Released in 1977, the book quickly sold twenty thousand copies. Jenner also traveled the country and world, in demand as a speaker, commanding $5,000 per appearance. Her appearance schedule became so packed that Jenner learned to fly a plane in order to get where she needed to

In 1977, Jenner became a spokesperson for Wheaties cereal, the so-called Breakfast of Champions.

be on time. She purchased a 1978 Beechcraft Bonanza airplane, took flying lessons, and got her ratings as a pilot.

Although she hadn't been chosen for the Superman role, Jenner landed a spot in another movie, the 1980 musical comedy *Can't Stop the Music*. There, Jenner starred alongside actor Valerie Perrine and the popular 1970s disco group the Village People. The film was loosely based on the Village People's formation. In the film, Jenner played the character of Ron White, a lawyer who represents the group. Harshly reviewed by critics, audiences stayed away and the film flopped. For her work, Jenner was nominated

Jenner appears alongside costar Valerie Perrine (left) and director Nancy Walker (right) at a promotional event for *Can't Stop the Music* in June 1980.

for a Razzie, an award presented at the annual Golden Raspberry Awards to the worst actor.

Undeterred by the film's performance, Jenner appeared on numerous television shows and specials from an ice-skating special with Olympic figure skater Dorothy Hamill to hosting the first National Collegiate Cheerleading Championship. Chrystie appeared in a small

NATIONAL CENTER FOR TRANSGENDER EQUALITY

The National Center for Transgender Equality (NCTE) is the country's leading social justice advocacy organization for members of the transgender community. Founded in 2003, the NCTE advocates for transgender rights at the local, state, and federal levels, working to change laws, policies, and societal attitudes. It educates members of Congress on issues that affect the transgender community and serves as an expert resource on transgender issues. Issues that the NCTE works on include employment discrimination, fair housing, hate crimes and violence, unequal treatment and sexual violence, limited access to health care, bullying and harassment in schools, and limited access to sex-specific bathrooms and locker rooms.

part in a made-for-television movie. Even the Jenners' dog, Bertha, landed a dog-food contract with General Mills.

THE PERSONAL TOLL OF FAME

In the first few years after Montreal, Jenner accepted almost every offer that came her way, from commercials and television shows to motivational speeches. In 1977 alone, Jenner earned an estimated $500,000, which would be worth about $2 million in 2015. Jenner explained her motivation to work hard immediately after Montreal in a November 1980 article in *Sports Illustrated*, saying, "This is why I worked so hard at first. When the Games ended on the evening of July 30, 1976, when I had won my medal, I figured that I had four years from that moment to learn a trade. Four years and no more, because when the next Olympic champion came along he'd obviously take my spot as the...whatever you want to call it, as the sports hero I was."

Yet while she was putting herself in the public eye at every turn, Jenner knew that she was still hiding her deepest secret. At appearances, she would wear a bra and pantyhose underneath a suit, without anyone knowing the truth. She felt like a liar and was frustrated that she couldn't tell the whole story about who she really was. Instead of feeling satisfied with her success, Jenner felt totally empty inside.

In 1978, the Jenners welcomed their first child, Burt, named after Caitlyn Jenner's late brother who had died in a car crash four months after the Olympics. While many families might consider settling down after having their first child, the hectic pace of Jenner's schedule soon took a toll on her marriage. Speaking engagements, public appearances, and television filming kept Jenner away from home twenty days a month, while Chrystie spent most of her time alone with the baby. A year later, they had grown too far apart. Jenner and Chrystie separated in late 1979, after seven years of marriage. At the time, Chrystie was two months pregnant with their daughter, Cassandra. Their divorce became final in 1981, and Jenner took a house a couple of miles away in Malibu.

CHAPTER 4

DIFFICULT DECISIONS

Four years after the Montreal Olympics, Jenner had become a household name. She'd earned enough money to be financially secure. Now she could pick and choose the projects that she wanted to work on. In a November 1980 article with *Sports Illustrated*, Jenner explained the changes, saying, "I run my own life these days. Funny, but I've found that my perspective has changed. Now, four years after the gold medal, I don't want to be seen quite as much. I don't know, perhaps I shouldn't be seen as much." Balancing her time in and out of the spotlight would remain a major part of Jenner's life for years to come.

A SECOND CHANCE AT LOVE

In 1979, while separated from first wife Chrystie, Jenner attended a celebrity tennis tournament at the Playboy Mansion (the home of Hugh Hefner, founder of the adult magazine *Playboy*). When Jenner won the tournament, an attractive young woman named Linda Thompson, handed her the trophy. Thompson was a Memphis, Tennessee, beauty queen and fledgling actress who had a recurring role on *Hee Haw*, a television variety show. She had been dating rock singer Elvis Presley when Jenner was competing in the 1976 Olympics. Upon meeting in 1979, she remembered the athlete, and now Thompson was single. The two hit it off immediately, and Thompson accepted Jenner's invitation to dinner. They started dating almost immediately.

A few months later in 1980, Thompson was thrilled to learn that she was pregnant. Once Jenner's divorce from Chrystie Crownover was complete, Jenner and Thompson decided to get married. On January 5, 1981, the two married at the beachfront Hawaiian home of Alan Carr, producer of *Can't Stop the Music*. About thirty-five people attended the wedding, including the couple's parents and

Linda Thompson was Jenner's second wife. The couple married on January 5, 1981.

Jenner's two-year-old son Burt. Together, they said their vows as the sun set over the Pacific Ocean.

On June 4, 1981, Brandon Thompson Jenner was born. Jenner's two older children, Burt and Cassandra, came to the hospital to visit their new little brother. Two years later, Jenner and Thompson welcomed a second son, Sam Brody Jenner.

Brandon and Brody Jenner stand outside a movie premiere in Westwood, California, on July 1, 1997.

BACK INTO THE SPOTLIGHT

Undeterred by the poor reception *Can't Stop the Music* received, Jenner continued to pursue an acting career. In 1981, she appeared as Jim Gregory in *Grambling's White Tiger*, a made-for-television movie about a white quarterback who attends a historically black college and deals with resentment. Also in 1981, Jenner landed a recurring role as Officer Steve McLeish for six episodes on the hit cop show *CHiPs*. Over the next several years, she also made appearances on several other television shows, including *The Fall Guy*, *Murder She Wrote*, and *The Love Boat*. Still, Hollywood stardom remained elusive.

During those years, Jenner became fascinated with another type of competition, driving a racecar. After competing in and winning several celebrity races, Jenner began to enter professional races. "[Jenner] worked really hard at it and had good natural ability," said friend and fellow driver Scott Pruett in a February 2015 article in the *New York Daily News*. He continued (using masculine pronouns), "He knew, with his background, he was in great shape; he had the ability to jump in a car and go drive and be on his game for hours."

Between 1980 and 1988, Jenner entered nearly sixty racing events across the country. Many of them were endurance races, which lasted between three and twenty-four hours. This type of race tests the drivers' limits, as they switch in shifts behind the wheel with their racing partners. Jenner raced with professionals such as Pruett, typically using Ford cars at tracks on the International Motor Sports Association

TRANSGENDER PIONEER: CHRISTINA KAHRL

Forty-seven-year-old Christina Kahrl has been fighting for transgender rights since she publicly transitioned in 2003. Like Jenner, Kahrl is active in the sports community. She is the cofounder of Baseball Prospectus, a sports analytics website, and a baseball writer and editor. Kahrl says that her passion for baseball and knowledge of the sport has helped her find common ground with other sports fans. Since her transition, she has received respect and acceptance from family, friends, and colleagues. Kahrl considers herself lucky, as many transgender people are rejected by family and friends, harassed at work and school, discriminated against when it comes to finding housing, and face physical and sexual abuse. Kahrl promotes her own story as an example of how transgender people can flourish and succeed when given the same opportunities and respect as cisgender members of society.

circuit. Jenner compared racing to the decathlon, noting that racing took a lot of timing, guts, and judgment.

REVELATIONS

During their marriage, Jenner and Thompson appeared to be the perfect couple. Athletic and good-looking, the pair were red-carpet regulars and were often photographed on the beach playing with their two young sons. They enjoyed many of the same activities, including jet skiing, water skiing, and tennis. The couple also supported several charities, serving as the national honorary chairpersons of the Juvenile Diabetes Association and regularly supporting the Special Olympics.

For Thompson, the marriage was perfect, and she had no idea that her spouse was struggling with gender dysphoria. In an April 2015 article for the Huffington Post, Thompson recalled (using masculine pronouns) that Jenner "possessed such a natural athleticism in everything he attempted to do. He seemed to excel in every sport he tried. Whatever he did, he was daring and cut an amazing form. [Jenner] was pretty much the perfect specimen of a man." She continued, "Men aspired to be like him and wanted to hang out and play sports with him, and women were clearly attracted to him. The Bruce [the name Jenner was given at birth] I knew back then was unstudied, affable, and seemingly very comfortable in his own skin. So it seemed."

So Thompson was stunned when one day in 1985, Jenner came to her and revealed that she identified as female. At first, Thompson was confused and did not understand what Jenner meant. Jenner explained that for as long as she could remember, she had felt like a woman on the inside, even though she had been assigned male at birth. Jenner explained to Thompson that she felt as if she had lived in the wrong skin and the wrong body for her entire life. Now, she wanted to move forward with transitioning. Thompson was stunned. She had never seen any signs over the years that Jenner struggled with gender dysphoria. Unlike Jenner's first wife, Thompson hadn't even been aware that Jenner liked to dress in women's clothing in secret.

Thompson suggested that the couple go to therapy. She wanted to understand Jenner's issues and find out if it was something that could be overcome. "I was naïve," she wrote. "As I said, I was pretty ignorant of the fact that being transgender isn't something that can be overcome, fixed, prayed away, exorcised or obliterated by any other arcane notion. Being transgender, like being gay, tall, short, white, black, male, or female, is another part of the human condition that makes each individual unique, and something over which we have no control. We are who we are in the deepest recesses of our minds, hearts and identities. I had to learn that

While married to her second wife, Linda, Caitlyn Jenner first sought treatment for gender dysphoria and considered transitioning.

life lesson and apply it to my own expectations for my future and the future of my family."

The couple went to see Dr. Gertrude Hill, a therapist who specialized in gender dysphoria. Hill calmly explained to Thompson that gender identity is not a phase—that Jenner's identity was that of a woman. Furthermore, Hill told Thompson that she had a choice to make: to either stay with Jenner as she transitioned or to separate. At the time, Jenner was considering traveling to another county to have gender affirmation surgery, after which she could return to the United States and live openly as a woman.

After six months of therapy, the couple separated. For Thompson, being married to a woman was not what she wanted for her life. She kept Jenner's secret private. When asked about the breakup, Thompson blamed Jenner's work schedule and long periods away from home.

BEGINNING TO TRANSITION

The mid- to late 1980s were a dark time for Jenner. Her professional opportunities began to diminish, and she was tired of giving motivational speeches. Her acting career had never really taken off. And in her personal life, two marriages had failed. She was running out of new and exciting professional opportunities. Furthermore, her gender dysphoria was getting stronger. Aware of her gender identity, Jenner began the process of transitioning.

Jenner began to take female sex hormones and had plastic surgery on her nose. She also underwent painful electrolysis procedures to remove hair from her face and chest. Electrolysis targeted one hair at a time with an electrical current. The hormones caused her to grow breasts. One day, her son Brody saw her get out of the shower and later told his mother that Jenner had boobs. Thompson explained the changes to Brody by saying that some of Jenner's chest muscle must have gotten flabby. Although Thompson knew the truth, she kept Jenner's gender identity a secret for many years out of respect for Jenner's privacy, not even telling her sons until they were thirty-one and twenty-nine years old, respectively.

Rumors about Jenner's changing appearance surfaced in the media. Jenner was terrified at the truth being discovered. At the time, there were few public figures living openly as transgender. Although Jenner was growing comfortable with herself, she was not ready to come out as transgender to the public. She dated several heterosexual women even as she continued to privately transition.

The internal struggles that weighed on Jenner affected her relationship with her children. She was distant to Burt, Cassandra, Brandon, and Brody. Jenner missed many milestones in her children's lives, from birthdays to graduations. Sometimes, two or three years would go by during which Jenner would not contact her children. In a July 2015 article in Vanity Fair, Jenner admits that she has regrets about her relationship with her children. "I have made a lot of mistakes raising the four Jenner kids. I had times not only dealing with my own issues but exes. [It was] very traumatic and there was a lot of turmoil in my life, and I wasn't as close to my kids as I should have been."

CHAPTER 5

REALITY STAR

Around 1990, Jenner felt as if she had been drifting. Her Olympic success was years in the past, and her life since was marked by two failed marriages and a disappointing acting career. She had worked very hard for two decades but felt that she had little to show for it. She decided to stop her transition; the timing wasn't yet right. Around the same time, Jenner met Kris Kardashian.

Kris Kardashian, a thirty-four-year-old former flight attendant, had just ended her marriage to lawyer Robert Kardashian, who famously defended O.J. Simpson in his murder trial. Kris's friend Candace Garvey (the wife of major league baseball player Steve Garvey) suggested that Kardashian

Kris Kardashian attends an event in Century City, California, on December 10, 1990.

and Jenner meet. At first, neither Kardashian nor Jenner was interested. Kardashian wanted to focus on raising her four young children after her divorce. Jenner, who preferred to dress in leisurely track suits, was also hesitant when Garvey described Kardashian as someone who was into fashion and shopping. However, Jenner was intrigued when she found out that Kardashian also had four children. Here was someone who came with as much baggage as I do, she thought.

Eventually, Jenner and Kardashian agreed to a blind date. They met the Garveys for drinks at the Riviera Country Club in Los Angeles. The two immediately connected. The next day, Jenner flew to Florida for a speaking engagement, but the pair talked on the phone repeatedly. From that moment on, they became inseparable. Once Kardashian's divorce from her husband Robert was finalized, Jenner and Kris married in an elegant ceremony in the ritzy neighborhood of Bel Air, Los Angeles, on April 21, 1991, just seven months after they first met.

BLENDING FAMILIES

At first, the couple appeared to be successfully merging Jenner's four children and the four Kardashians—Kourtney, Kimberly, Khloe, and

Robert Jr.—into a happy, blended family. The eight children performed together at their parents' wedding. The Jenner children lived with their mothers but frequently visited the Jenner-Kardashian household for meals and weekends.

However, not long after the wedding, the invitations for the Jenner children stopped coming. The relationship between Jenner and Kardashian and the Jenner children and Jenner's ex-wives became increasingly strained. Slowly, Jenner slipped from her children's lives. According to Burt Jenner, he does not remember seeing his parent more than twice a year for a period of about ten years. Jenner later admitted that, at the time, she was focused on her four stepchildren and the two new daughters she had with Kardashian—Kendall (born in 1995) and Kylie (born in 1997)—at the expense of her four oldest children. She maintained that she would have an easier time building a relationship with the Jenner children once they were older and no longer living with their mothers.

Meanwhile, Kris Kardashian took the initiative to reboot Jenner's career. Before they met, Jenner had been living paycheck to paycheck. Now Kardashian fired Jenner's handlers, and she herself became Jenner's manager. She revived Jenner's speaking engagements,

Pictured is the Jenner-Kardashian family with the four children from Caitlyn Jenner's first two marriages and Kris's four children from her previous marriage to Robert Kardashian. The couple would later go on to have two more daughters together.

raising her fees. She negotiated endorsement deals and promoted Jenner's racing career. She booked Jenner on infomercials for Eagle Eyes Sunglasses and launched new business ventures in aircraft supplies. Jenner and Kardashian even appeared together in an infomercial series for workout equipment. Their efforts paid off financially for the family.

TEEN ACTIVIST: JAZZ JENNINGS

From the moment she could talk, Jazz Jennings (who had been assigned male at birth) told her parents that she was a girl. At age five, she became one of the youngest people in the world diagnosed with gender dysphoria. At age six, she and her parents went public with her story, appearing with Barbara Walters on the ABC News program *20/20*. Even at six years old, Jazz knew that she wanted to help other kids like herself. As a teenager, Jazz continued to advocate for transgender youth. She cowrote a children's book, *I Am Jazz*, published in 2014, and she also starred in a reality show of the same name on the Learning Channel (TLC). Through her YouTube channel, Jazz became influential offering encouragement to other trans children and teenagers. For her work, Jazz was named one of *Time* magazine's 25 Most Influential Teens of 2014.

KEEPING UP WITH THE KARDASHIANS

When family friend Kathie Lee Gifford suggested that the Kardashian-Jenner family would be perfect for reality television, Kris Kardashian met with Ryan Seacrest, the host of reality show *American Idol*, who owned his own production company. *The Osbournes*, a reality show that followed the family of rock star Ozzy Osbourne, was popular at the time, and Seacrest wanted to do something similar. He hired a cameraman to go to the Kardashians' house and shoot a family barbeque they were having on Sunday. The family was as crazy and fun-loving as ever, and Seacrest knew he was on to something. He pitched the idea for the show to executives at the E! Network, a cable network known for its entertainment and reality programming. The network gave Seacrest the green light to move forward with the show.

In August 2007, the E! Network announced that the Kardashian and Jenner family would star in a new reality show. The Kardashians—namely mom Kris and children Kourtney, Kim, Khloe, Rob, Kendall, and Kylie—were all excited to star in the new show. Jenner, however, was not so sure. In 2003, she had participated in a celebrity reality show titled *I'm a Celebrity, Get Me Out of*

The four Kardashian children pose together at the premiere of their reality television show *Keeping Up with the Kardashians* on October 9, 2007, in Los Angeles, California.

Here! She had no desire to do it again and relive the reality circus. She initially refused to participate in the show. Eventually, however, she was convinced to go along with it.

The first episode of *Keeping Up with the Kardashians* aired on October 14, 2007. It featured Jenner pulling a then ten-year-old Kylie away from a stripper pole. The show focused on the lives of the Kardashian-Jenner family and the antics of the Kardashian daughters. Subsequent episodes featured everything from visits to a nail salon to plastic surgery and exotic vacations in Bora Bora. Jenner's son Brody appeared in a few episodes, along with other friends and acquaintances of the family.

RAKING IN VIEWERS AND DOLLARS

The show was a success with viewers from the beginning. In its first month on air, 1.3 million total viewers tuned in, and *Keeping Up with the Kardashians* quickly became the highest-rated series on Sunday nights for adults aged eighteen to thirty-four. In a November 2007 article published in the *New York Daily News*, Lisa Berger, the executive vice president of original programming and series development for E!, said, "The buzz surrounding the series is huge, and viewers have clearly fallen for the Kardashians. Seacrest and Bunim-Murray's unique ability to capture this family's one-of-a-kind dynamics and hilarious antics has made the series a fantastic addition to our prime-time lineup."

Critics panned the show, calling it a show about desperate women grasping at fame. Others complained that it was boring to watch the family go about their daily lives and criticized them for using the show to gain celebrity. Despite the critical reviews, audiences continued to tune in each week to watch the family's exploits, squabbles, and dramas. In 2010, the show's season five premiere pulled in 4.67 million viewers, its most watched episode ever.

Keeping Up with the Kardashians was nominated for—and won—several television awards. It has been nominated for the Teen Choice Awards Choice TV: Reality Show category every year since 2008, winning three times. The show won a People's Choice Award for Favorite TV Guilty Pleasure in 2011. In 2010, Kris Kardashian and Caitlyn Jenner were nominated for a Teen Choice Award for Choice TV Parental Unit. The Kardashian sisters have also been nominated and won several Teen Choice Awards for Choice TV: Reality/Variety Star.

The show was a financial goldmine for the family. In 2015, Kris Kardashian signed a deal to renew the show for four new seasons that was rumored to be worth up to $100 million. In addition, the show's success led to lucrative endorsements, clothing and perfume lines, and mobile apps for the family.

Amid all of the show's antics, Jenner was not spotted frequently. When she did appear, she was often portrayed as the stock character of a bumbling, out-of-touch parent. A new generation saw the Olympic champion as a pushover.

Entire storylines seemed designed to make Jenner look foolish, such as one episode in which Kris Kardashian refused to give Jenner five hundred dollars to repair a toy helicopter and took away Jenner's ATM card to make sure she didn't spend the money. Jenner was forced to change light bulbs and clean for Khloe in order to borrow money.

Year after year, Jenner played her part on the reality show. All the while, she knew that she was hiding the real story from everyone around her. In her April 2015 interview with Diane Sawyer, Jenner shared, "The entire run, I kept thinking to myself, 'Oh my God, this whole thing, the one real, true story in the family was the one I was hiding and nobody knew about it.' The one thing that could make a difference in people's lives was right here in my soul and I could not tell that story." By 2013, Jenner had grown increasingly unhappy. She needed to make a change in her life.

CHAPTER 6

MAKING THE TRANSITION

Although they appeared to have it all—fame, fortune, and a beautiful family—the Jenners' marriage had slowly begun to disintegrate. As the family's reality show became a hit and the money poured in, Caitlin Jenner says that she felt like Kris Kardashian no longer needed her, that Kardashian was running the show and had her own financial security. The couple drifted further apart as Kardashian tended to the expanding family empire.

An October 2013 article in *People* magazine alleged that Kardashian ran everything at home. The anonymous source claimed that

Kris Jenner and her three elder daughters (left) appear at an E! Entertainment promotional event in April 2012. The following year, Kris and Caitlyn Jenner would announce their separation to the public.

Jenner "basically had no say in anything. [Jenner] was told what to do. You'd go over [to their house] and there were always a million people running around, and it was pretty obvious [Jenner] didn't feel comfortable in [the] house anymore." Although Jenner was famous in her own right when she married Kris, she was uncomfortable with the spotlight the new show had put on their lives. Jenner felt as if the walls were closing in on her.

MOVE TO MALIBU

In 2013, Jenner's stepdaughter Kim Kardashian announced that, while her own home was being renovated, she and her boyfriend, the rapper and record producer Kanye West, would be moving back into the Jenner-Kardashian family home. Caitlyn Jenner knew that it was time to leave.

Jenner, along with daughters Kendall and Kylie (who also felt cramped at home), rented a beach house in Malibu, living there for the entire summer. When summer ended, the girls returned home, but Jenner stayed. Malibu had become a peaceful escape from the harsh glare of fame and the humiliations she faced at home.

In October 2013, Jenner and Kardashian officially announced their separation. Filmed for an episode of *Keeping Up with the Kardashians*, Jenner and Kardashian held a family meeting in which Jenner explained that the couple would no longer live in the same house. The kids were upset by the announcement. Kendall cried, and Khloe got visibly mad, but the children all eventually accepted the new living arrangement.

Jenner and Kardashian put on a cheerful face for the public about their separation. In a joint statement, they explained that they were happier living apart but would always love and respect each other. They also said that their family would remain their first priority.

More than a year later, Kardashian filed for divorce citing "irreconcilable differences" as the reason for their split. The couple completed the divorce without lawyers and agreed to split their assets. Jenner kept the contracts that were hers, while Kardashian kept hers, including all business interests and intellectual property related to *Keeping Up with the Kardashians* and its various spin-offs.

FURTHER CHANGES

Now living alone, Jenner started hormone therapy once again in 2014. She also began to make subtle changes to her appearance. She grew her hair longer, often wearing it in a low ponytail. When Kardashian had always demanded that she cut it, Jenner refused and got highlights. The paparazzi snapped pictures of Jenner whenever they had the chance, noting her earrings, nail polish, and lip-gloss. Soon, the tabloids were overly intrusive and sensationalizing the changes in Jenner's appearance.

Jenner ignored the tabloids and refused to address questions about her appearance. In December 2013, Jenner had planned to undergo a tracheal shave, a common procedure for trans women. She cancelled the procedure after word leaked to tabloid reporters and any hope of privacy vanished. One night after tabloids reported the cancelled procedure, Jenner paced in her Malibu home. She thought about committing suicide, unsure if she could withstand the pressure of the paparazzi and public eye. Many members of the trans community must confront such feelings, which are difficult to handle even when one isn't a celebrity. (If you or anybody you know ever feels depressed or is considering suicide, reach out for help. Trans Lifeline is a free, anonymous hotline staffed by transgender people who can help you. Its numbers are [877] 565-8860 [in the United States] and [877] 330-6366 [in Canada.]) However, Jenner decided not to go through with a suicide attempt. Instead, it was time to start telling the truth.

Jenner rescheduled the appointment for her tracheal shave with another doctor in February 2014. Once again, a tabloid found out and photographed her leaving the doctor's office with a bandage over her throat. Immediately, the media exploded in a frenzy, speculating on Jenner's gender identity.

FATAL ACCIDENT

In February 2015, Jenner was involved in a multiple-vehicle accident that killed one person and injured several others. While driving in Malibu, Jenner's SUV rear-ended a Lexus that had stopped behind another car. The impact pushed the Lexus into traffic on the Pacific Coast Highway, where it was hit by another car. The Lexus's driver was pronounced dead at the scene. After an investigation, the Los Angeles County Sheriff's Department found that Jenner was driving too fast for the rain-slickened conditions. However, the sheriff decided not to file manslaughter charges against Jenner because she was not driving recklessly or at an excessive speed, had not fled the scene, was not using a cell phone at the time of the accident, and was traveling with the flow of traffic. The accident brought further unwanted media attention to Jenner's life during a difficult time.

COMING OUT TO HER FAMILY

Throughout her life, Jenner confided in very few people about her gender dysphoria. Most people in her life did not know about

Jenner's gender identity, including her family. The stories in the tabloids, however, made her realize that she was going to have to tell her children and her family sooner rather than later about her plans to transition. She also decided to come up with a strategy for announcing her transition to the public.

Over the years, the Kardashian and Jenner children had some awareness of Jenner's habit of dressing in women's clothing, but it was not a topic that was discussed openly. One time, stepdaughter Kim had come home and caught Jenner completely dressed as a woman in the garage, wearing full clothing, heels, makeup, and a wig. Kim ran to her car and quickly drove away. Later, Jenner called Kim to make sure that she was OK, but they never talked about the incident again.

Another time, Jenner's daughter Kendall set up a computer video camera in her room because she thought her sister Kylie was borrowing her clothes without permission. Any movement in Kendall's bedroom activated the camera. When she reviewed the video later, Kendall saw her father trying on a dress. Still, neither of them discussed what she had seen.

Now Jenner knew that it was time to be honest with the people she loved the most. However, she was afraid of their reactions. "I was terrified to tell the children," she revealed in her April 2015 interview with Diane Sawyer. "Every single one of them. I can't let myself hurt them. How do I do this and not hurt my children?"

She told each child, beginning with Brandon, who said that he had never been more proud of his father than he was at that moment. For the four elder Jenner children, the news was not a complete surprise. Burt and Cassandra's mother had told them about Jenner's gender identity when they were thirteen and eleven years old, respectively. Brandon had suspected the truth because of the physical changes he witnessed in Jenner. Brody learned about Jenner's gender identity from his mother when he was twenty-nine years old. Learning the truth was almost a relief for him. Knowing that Jenner was dealing with her own issues helped Brody understand why she had missed out on a lot of his childhood milestones. When Cassandra asked what Jenner wanted the kids to call her, she told them to keep calling her "dad" because that's who she had always been to them.

In early 2015, Jenner gathered Kendall, Kylie, Kim, Kourtney, and Khloe to reveal his truth to them. The girls had noticed Jenner's physical changes and had been wondering what was going on with their father. It was time to be honest and open with them. They gathered for a family meeting at Kourtney Kardashian's house. Jenner got right to the point, explaining to them that she was a woman. After their initial surprise, the girls rallied around Jenner. Daughters Kendall and Kylie released a statement to ABC News in April 2015 saying, "We love our dad very much as he is an amazing father. We couldn't ask for a better dad. He has the biggest heart and all we want for him is to be happy. If he's happy, we're happy."

For Kim, invaluable advice came from husband Kanye West. In Jenner's April 2015 interview with Diane Sawyer, Jenner recounted the conversation, saying, "They were talking about it and [Kanye] says to Kim, 'Look, I can be married to the most beautiful woman in the world, and I am. I can have the most beautiful little daughter in the world. I have that. But I'm nothing if I can't be me...if I can't be true to myself, they don't mean anything.'...and since then, Kimberly has been, by far, the most accepting, and the easiest to talk to."

Kim Kardashian and Kanye West appear together at the Metropolitan Museum of Art in New York City, New York, on May 4, 2015. As Caitlyn Jenner's son-in-law, West would make a strong show of public support for Jenner's transition.

COMPLETING THE TRANSITION

Now that she had discussed her plans with her family, Jenner was ready to complete her transition. She was already taking hormones and had hair on her body and face removed. She had also already had plastic surgery on her nose and a tracheal shave. At that point, in March 2015, she headed to the office of a surgeon who specialized in facial feminization surgery (FFS). This type of surgery involves procedures such as hairline correction, forehead contouring, and jaw and chin contouring. She would also have a breast augmentation procedure. (Note that some transgender individuals seek surgical intervention so that their physical appearance is perceived by societal standards to match more closely their gender identity; others do not, either because they do not feel this is necessary, they seek to challenge societal standards of gender expression, or because such procedures are cost prohibitive. Such procedures are not a necessary part of a person's transition.)

About ten hours after surgery, Jenner left the surgeon's office. Recuperating from the surgeries was painful, and Jenner was on large doses of pain medication. At one point, she had a panic

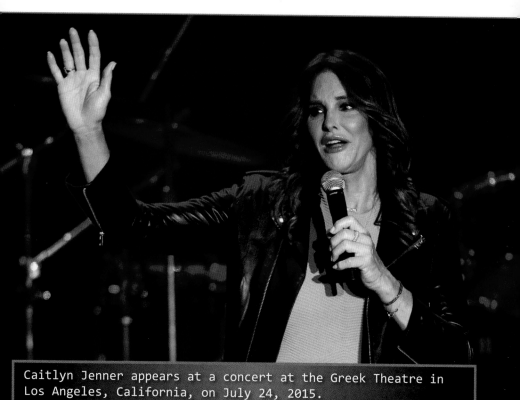

Caitlyn Jenner appears at a concert at the Greek Theatre in Los Angeles, California, on July 24, 2015.

attack, something that had never happened before in her life. She told the twenty-four-hour nurse on watch that she needed to get out of bed. Jenner walked to the long hallway in her home and paced back and forth until the panic attack subsided. During the attack, she questioned what she had done.

A counselor for the Los Angeles Gender Center arrived at the house to talk to Jenner and ease her mind. The counselor reassured her that panic attacks were commonly brought on by the pain medication she was taking. She also told Jenner that second-guessing her decision was a common—and usually temporary—reaction after gender affirmation surgery. After that, Jenner's concerns eased, and she never regretted her decision again. In a July 2015 article in Vanity Fair, she explained, "If I was lying on my deathbed and I had kept this secret and never ever did anything about it, I would be lying there saying, 'You just blew your entire life.'"

Once she had told her family about her transition, it was time to go public. In the months immediately prior to coming out to her family, media scrutiny around Jenner had intensified, as tabloids speculated about her gender identity and rumored transition. Such invasive sensationalism can make transgender figures feel ridiculed in the public eye. Jenner, however, did not want to be ridiculed; she saw an opportunity to inspire others once again and be a role model. To set the matter straight, Jenner agreed to sit down for an interview with Diane Sawyer that would be broadcast nationally on ABC News.

CHAPTER 7

I AM CAIT

Ready to tell the world her truth, Jenner sat down with Diane Sawyer in early 2015. Over several hours and interviews in both New York and California, Jenner talked to Sawyer about the gender dysphoria she had been fighting since childhood. The two-hour interview aired on national television as a special edition of ABC News' *20/20* news program on April 24, 2015. Jenner put the rumors about her changing appearance to rest quickly, telling Sawyer, "For all intents and purposes, I'm a woman." From that day on, Jenner could be her true self in the public eye. "I look at it this way—Bruce always telling a lie. He's lived a lie his whole life about who he is. And I can't do that any longer," Jenner said in the interview.

INTRODUCING CAITLYN

After sixty-five years of hiding her true self, Caitlyn Jenner appeared on the July 2015 cover of *Vanity Fair* magazine. In the magazine, she was featured in a lengthy twenty-two-page article written by Buzz Bissinger, a Pulitzer Prize–winning reporter. Famed photographer Annie Leibovitz snapped the photographs for the feature article that showed Jenner in full Hollywood glamour, draped in sexy gowns. On the cover, Jenner posed in a strapless, white bustier, with her face and hair flawlessly done.

In a *Vanity Fair* article published in the month prior to the Jenner feature, stylist Jessica Diehl talked about how she and Jenner chose the cover look. Diehl shared:

...There was a stripped-down idea there that sort of felt like underneath all of this excitement and newsworthiness is the soul of a woman. And that didn't need a lot of covering up. It was not meant to be risqué in any way. It was really meant to sort of show with all honesty and purity, "This is what is going on. Here I am."

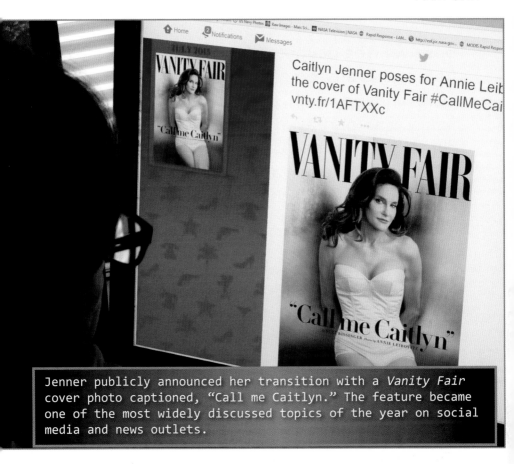

Jenner publicly announced her transition with a *Vanity Fair* cover photo captioned, "Call me Caitlyn." The feature became one of the most widely discussed topics of the year on social media and news outlets.

Around when the cover was revealed, Jenner started a Twitter account in her chosen name. She tweeted, "I'm so happy after such a long struggle to be living my true self. Welcome to the world Caitlyn. Can't wait for you to get to know her/me." Within hours, more than 1.1 million people followed her account.

Family, friends, and fans flooded the Internet with support. Most reactions were positive, with daughter Kendall tweeting, "Be free now pretty bird." Some family members were unhappy with the way the Kardashian family was portrayed in the *Vanity Fair* article. Kris Jenner and daughters Khloe and Kim were initially upset about Jenner's negative comments about Kris and their marriage in the article.

I AM CAIT

No longer burdened by her secret, Jenner was free to live her life openly. When she flew to New York City for Gay Pride weekend in June 2015, photographers followed her and snapped pictures as she shopped, attended Broadway shows, and went to dinner with friends. Her immediate sense of style impressed many. Christina Pacelli, stylist for *Orange Is the New Black* star Laverne Cox, commented that Jenner was carrying herself beautifully.

Jenner also announced that she would be starring in her own reality show, *I Am Cait*. The show would document her transition and follow her as she educated herself about transgender issues. The eight-episode documentary series debuted on July 26, 2015, on the E! Network, the same network that airs *Keeping Up with the Kardashians*. The show focused on Jenner's new life, her changing relationships with family and friends, and new friendships with a group of transgender women. The show also explored how Jenner was adjusting to being a role model for the transgender community because of her celebrity. While Jenner's ex-wife Kris and several of Jenner's children and stepchildren appeared on the show, the family drama was kept to a minimum. Instead, Jenner insisted that the show feature advocates that would address serious issues such as suicide in the transgender community.

For the first episode, 2.7 million viewers tuned in to watch. Critical reception of the show was generally positive. Critics praised the show for its sensitive approach to the social issues faced by the transgender community as well as its ability to help viewers see and understand transgender people. In one episode, Jenner met with fellow transgender celebrity Chaz Bono and attended a meeting of Transforming Family, a support group for trans youth and families in Los Angeles.

Although the press was positive, the ratings for the show were a disappointment. After

Caitlyn Jenner appears with her ex-wife Kris at the 2015 Victoria's Secret Fashion Show in New York City, New York, on November 10, 2015.

the premiere, ratings dropped by more than half. By the end of the season, they had stabilized with 1.3 million viewers watching the season finale in September. Despite the disappointing ratings, E! Network announced in October 2015 that *I Am Cait* had been renewed for a second season, which would air in 2016. "Caitlyn's story has ignited a global conversation on the transgender community on a scale that has never been seen before," Jeff Olde, E!'s executive vice president of programming and development, said in an October 2015 statement about the show's renewal.

HIGHER SUICIDE RATES

Attempted suicide rates are significantly higher for transgender people than other Americans. According to the 2011 National Transgender Discrimination Survey, 41 percent of transgender and gender non-conforming people have attempted suicide, compared to the national average of 4.6 percent. Advocates believe that the discrimination and stigma faced by transgender people contribute to the higher suicide rate. In addition, the survey found that race further affected suicide rates in the transgender community, with multiracial (54 percent) and American Indian or Alaska

sidebar continued on the next page

Sidebar continued from the previous page

Native (56 percent) members of the transgender community being more likely to attempt suicide than whites (38 percent).

Financial stability is also a factor in suicide rates in the transgender community. Transgender respondents that were more financially stable were less likely to attempt suicide, while those making less than $10,000 annually were the most likely to attempt suicide (54 percent). Unemployment was another factor, with unemployed transgender people being more likely to attempt suicide (50 percent) than transgender people with a job (37 percent).

"We are honored Caitlyn has chosen to continue to share her ongoing story with our viewers around the world."

ARTHUR ASHE COURAGE AWARD

In July 2015, Caitlyn Jenner accepted the prestigious Arthur Ashe Courage Award at ESPN's ESPY Awards. The Courage Award is presented annually to individuals whose contributions "transcend sports." Past recipients include Muhammad Ali and Billie Jean King. As she walked to the podium to accept the award, the audience, which included

Jenner accepts the Arthur Ashe Courage Award at the 2015 ESPYs.

many of the world's biggest sports stars, gave her a standing ovation.

In her ten-minute acceptance speech, Jenner thanked her family and friends, and admitted that her transition has been harder than she could have imagined. She said that until earlier that year, she had never even met another transgender person. She promised to use her celebrity platform to reshape how transgender people are viewed and treated. The audience listened spellbound as Jenner spoke of transgender teens who are bullied, beaten up, commit suicide, or are murdered. She urged the audience—iconic sports figures—to give transgender people respect and to remember that what they say and do is watched by millions of people. "My plea for you tonight is…join me in making this one of your issues as well," she said. "If you want to call me names, make jokes and doubt my intentions, go ahead, because the reality is I can take it. But for thousands of kids out there coming to terms with the reality of who they are, they shouldn't have to take it."

Reaction to Jenner's winning the Courage Award was mixed. Many were proud of her and called her decision to come out as transgender extremely brave. Others were less supportive, suggesting that others had been more deserving of the award.

BECOMING AN ADVOCATE

In her interview with Diane Sawyer, Jenner said that she was uncomfortable at being thrust into a role of becoming an advocate for the transgender community simply because of her fame and celebrity. But soon after, she hosted a dinner for six transgender women, most of whom had transitioned five-to-ten years earlier. Jenner realized that she did not know much about the problems they faced each day. She realized she could use her celebrity to highlight transgender issues that had been hidden for so long.

Her high-profile transition and electrifying speech at the ESPY Awards positioned her to become one of the most visible and recognized faces of the transgender community. Jenner's celebrity also focused a spotlight on the unique issues that the transgender community faces. She sparked a national conversation about how the media and people should treat and talk about transgender people. Jennifer Finney Boylan, a transgender advocate and cochair of the board of GLAAD (Gay and Lesbian Alliance Against Defamation), says that it is impossible to hate someone whose personal story and struggles you know. In an October 2015 article in *Glamour* magazine, Boylan explained the impact Jenner is having for the transgender community, noting, "Thanks to Caitlyn Jenner, the stories of thousands and thousands of trans people—in all their glorious, messy, contradictory struggles—are at last becoming known."

At the same time, some people have not been fully supportive of Jenner as the face of the transgender community. Some believe that the focus on Jenner's physical transformation overshadows more important transgender issues. Others point out that her experience as a wealthy white woman and celebrity does not give her the insight into the everyday struggles of transgender people of color, those with disabilities, or those who struggle financially. Without these experiences, some question whether Jenner can advocate effectively for the best interests of the entire transgender community.

While Jenner's work as a transgender celebrity advocate began relatively late in life, Jenner has repeatedly said that she feels happier now than she has been in a long time. Family and friends have noticed the changes, with daughter Kylie saying that she and her dad connect more now that Jenner has come out. Jenner was even named one of *Glamour* magazine's Women of the Year in 2015. In the October 2015 article accompanying the announcement, Jenner shared, "I am just excited about the future for the first time in a long, long time. And that is a nice feeling to have....To be honest with you, if the worst thing in the world that happens to you is you are trans, you've got it made."

TIMELINE

October 28, 1949 Caitlyn Marie Jenner is born in Mount Kisco, New York.

1968 Jenner attends Graceland College in Lamoni, Iowa.

1971 Jenner wins the decathlon at the Kansas Relays.

1972 Jenner competes in the 1972 Summer Olympics in Munich, Germany. She finishes in tenth place. Upon returning from the Olympics, Jenner marries her girlfriend, Chrystie Crownover.

1973 Jenner moves to San Jose, California, to train for the 1976 Olympics.

1975 Jenner wins the 1975 Pan American Games.

1976 Jenner wins the Olympic gold medal in the men's decathlon, breaking the world record.

1977 Jenner becomes a spokesperson for Wheaties brand breakfast cereal and appears on the Wheaties cereal box.

1979 Jenner and her wife, Chrystie Crownover, separate. They later divorce in 1981.

1979 Jenner meets her second wife, Linda Thompson.

1980 Jenner stars in *Can't Stop the Music*.

1980s Jenner's passion for racing emerges. Throughout the decade, she enters nearly sixty racing events across the country.

1985 Jenner reveals to wife Linda Thompson that she identifies as a woman. The couple enters counseling but separates after six months.

Late 1980s Jenner first attempts to transition but ultimately decides not to follow through.

1990 Jenner is introduced to Kris Kardashian. The pair immediately hit it off.

1991 Jenner marries Kris Kardashian.

2007 *Keeping Up with the Kardashians* premieres on the E! television network.

2013 Jenner moves out of the Kardashian-Jenner family home. She and Kris officially announce their separation.

2014 Jenner restarts hormone therapy and undergoes a tracheal shave.

Early 2015 Jenner reveals to her family that she is a trans woman.

April 2015 Jenner makes her transition public in a nationally broadcast interview on *20/20*.

June 2015 Jenner appears on the cover of the July issue of *Vanity Fair* magazine.

July 2015 A reality show documenting Jenner's transition, called *I Am Cait*, debuts. That same month, Jenner is awarded the Arthur Ashe Courage Award.

GLOSSARY

ADVOCATE A person who publicly supports or recommends a particular cause or policy.

AFFABLE Someone who is good-natured and easy to talk to.

APPREHENSIVE Anxious or afraid that something bad is going to happen.

CISGENDER A person whose gender identity is consistent with the gender they were assigned at birth.

DISCRIMINATION Treating someone differently because of a class or group that the person belong to.

DYSLEXIA A learning disorder that is characterized by difficulty reading due to problems identifying speech sounds and learning how they relate to letters and words.

ELECTROLYSIS A technique that uses electric current to permanently remove hair.

ENDORSEMENT Giving one's approval to someone or something, often for money.

ENDURANCE The ability to sustain an activity over a long period of time.

FLOURISH To grow or develop well in a healthy environment.

FRENZY A state of uncontrolled excitement or behavior.

GENDER DYSPHORIA The unhappiness produced by an incongruity between one's gender identity (the gender that a person internally feels that they are) and their apparent physical sex (the physical traits with which they were born).

GENDER IDENTITY A person's internal sense of gender, often expressed through behavior, clothing, hairstyle, voice, or body characteristics.

HORMONES Chemical messengers in the body that trigger certain functions.

INTELLECTUAL PROPERTY Creations of the mind, such as inventions, literary and artistic works, designs, symbols, names, and images, that are used in business.

PANIC ATTACK A sudden feeling of acute and disabling anxiety.

PAPARAZZI Independent photographers who take pictures of athletes, entertainers, politicians, and other celebrities as they go about their daily routines.

TABLOID A newspaper or magazine that focuses on celebrity gossip.

TRACHEAL SHAVE A surgical procedure in which the size of a patient's Adam's apple is reduced.

TRANSGENDER A person whose gender identity is inconsistent with the gender they were assigned at birth.

TRANSSEXUAL An older term used in the medical community to designate transgender individuals who seek surgical intervention so that their body's anatomy corresponds to their gender identity.

FOR MORE INFORMATION

Canadian Professional Association for Transgender Health (CPATH)
201-1770 Fort Street
Victoria, BC V8R 1J5
Canada
(250) 592-6183
Website: http://www.cpath.ca/
home/?lang=en
CPATH is the largest national multidisci-
plinary, professional organization in the
world, working to support the health,
well-being, and dignity of trans and gender
diverse people.

COLAGE
3815 South Othello Street, Suite 100, #310
Seattle, WA 98118
(855) 4-COLAGE
Website: http://www.colage.org
COLAGE brings together people with LGBTQ
parents to support them as they become
leaders in the LGBTQ and ally communities.

Gay and Lesbian Alliance Against Defamation
(GLAAD)
104 West 29th Street, 4th Floor
New York, NY 10001
(212) 629-3322

Website: http://www.glaad.org
GLAAD promotes positive representations of LGBTQ individuals in the media and public discussion, working to ensure that the rights and dignity of the LGBTQ community are respected.

Gender Proud
E-mail: hello@genderproud.com
Website: http://www.genderproud.com
Founded by trans woman model Geena Rocero, Gender Proud's advocacy work is directed at expanding gender marker rights, helping transgender people change their legal documentation to match their chosen name and gender identity.

National Center for Transgender Equality (NCTE)
1400 16th Street NW, Suite 510
Washington, DC 20036
(202) 642-4542
Website: http://www.transequality.org
The National Center for Transgender Equality (NCTE) is the country's leading social justice advocacy organization for transgender people. NCTE advocates for transgender issues and works to change laws, policies, and societal attitudes.

PFLAG Canada
331 Cooper Street, Suite 200
Ottawa, ON K2P 0G5
Canada
(888) 530-6777
Website: https://www.pflagcanada.ca/en/
  index.html
PFLAG Canada is Canada's only national
  organization that helps all Canadians
  with issues of sexual orientation, gender
  identity, and gender expression. PFLAG
  Canada provides support, education, and
  resources.

Transgender Law Center
1629 Telegraph Avenue, Suite 400
Oakland, CA 94612
(415) 865-0176
Website: http://transgenderlawcenter.org
The Transgender Law Center works to
  change laws, policies, and attitudes so that
  all people can live safely, authentically, and
  free from discrimination regardless of their
  gender identity or expression.

TransYouth Family Allies (TYFA)
PO Box 1471
Holland, MI 49422

(888) 462-8932

Website: http://www.imatyfa.org

TYFA helps trans children and families by part-
nering with educators, service providers, and
communities to develop supportive environ-
ments in which gender may be expressed
and respected.

WEBSITES

Because of the changing nature of Internet
links, Rosen Publishing has developed an
online list of websites related to the subject
of this book. This site is updated regularly.
Please use this link to access the list:

http://www.rosenlinks.com/TGP/jenner

FOR FURTHER READING

Andrews, Arin. *Some Assembly Required: The Not-So-Secret Life of a Transgender Teen*. New York, NY: Simon & Schuster, 2014.

Beck, Kristin, and Anne Speckhard. *Warrior Princess: A U.S. Navy Seal's Journey to Coming Out Transgender*. McLean, VA: Advances Press, 2013.

Duron, Lori. *Raising My Rainbow: Adventures in Raising a Fabulous, Gender Creative Son*. New York, NY: Random House, 2013.

Ehrensaft, Diane. *Gender Born, Gender Made: Raising Healthy Gender-Nonconforming Children*. New York, NY: The Experiment, 2011.

Gino, Alex. *George*. New York, NY: Scholastic, 2015.

Herthel, Jessica, and Jazz Jennings. *I Am Jazz*. New York, NY: Dial Books, 2014.

Hill, Katie Rain. *Rethinking Normal: A Memoir in Transition*. New York, NY: Simon & Schuster, 2014.

Huegel, Kelly. *GLBTQ: The Survival Guide for Gay, Lesbian, Bisexual, Transgender, and Questioning Teens*. Minneapolis, MN: Free Spirit Publishing, 2011.

Kuklin, Susan. *Beyond Magenta: Transgender Teens Speak Out*. Somerville, MA: Candlewick, 2014.

Mock, Janet. *Redefining Realness: My Path to Womanhood, Identity, Love & So Much More*. New York, NY: Atria Books, 2014.

Nutt, Amy Ellis. *Becoming Nicole: The Transformation of an American Family*. New York, NY: Random House, 2015.

Pelleschi, Andrea. *Transgender Rights and Issues*. Edina, MN: ABDO, 2015.

Pepper, Rachel. *Transitions of the Heart: Stories of Love, Struggle and Acceptance by Mothers of Transgender and Gender Variant Children*. Berkeley, CA: Cleis Press, 2012.

Polonsky, Ami. *Gracefully Grayson*. New York, NY: Disney-Hyperion, 2014.

Shultz, Jackson Wright. *Trans/Portraits: Voices from Transgender Communities*. Lebanon, NH: Dartmouth College Press, 2015.

Tesla, Rylan Jay, et al. *The Gender Quest Workbook: A Guide for Teens and Young Adults Exploring Gender Identity*. Oakland, CA: Instant Help, 2015.

Thompson, Tamara. *Transgender People*. Farmington, MI: Greenhaven Press, 2015.

Whittington, Hillary. *Raising Ryland: Our Story of Parenting a Transgender Child with No Strings Attached*. New York, NY: HarperCollins, 2016.

BIBLIOGRAPHY

ABC News. "Bruce Jenner: The Interview." April 24, 2015.

Access Hollywood. "Ryan Seacrest Talks Kardashians, The Wanted & The Future Of American Idol." June 14, 2013 (www.accesshollywood.com/articles/ryan-seacrest-talks-kardashians-the-wanted-the-future-of-american-idol-133990).

Bentley, Jean, "Bruce Jenner Tells Diane Sawyer "I Am a Woman": Read the Complete Live Blog from Interview." *US Weekly*, April 24, 2015 (www.usmagazine.com/entertainment/news/bruce-jenner-interview-with-diane-sawyer-read-us-weeklys-live-blog-2015244).

Bissinger, Buzz, "Caitlyn Jenner: The Full Story." *Vanity Fair*, June 30, 2015 (www.vanityfair.com/hollywood/2015/06/caitlyn-jenner-bruce-cover-annie-leibovitz).

Blumm, K. C. "Bruce and Kris Jenner Split: What Went Wrong." *People*, October 9, 2013 (www.people.com/people/article/0,,20743440,00.html).

Cooper, Chet. "Gold Medalist Bruce Jenner Interviewed by Chet Cooper." *ABILITY*, August/September 1999 (http://www.abilitymagazine.com/jenner_interview.html).

Dooley, Sean, et al. "Bruce Jenner's Journey Through the Years." ABC News, April 24, 2015 (http://abcnews.go.com/Entertainment/bruce-jenners-journey-years/story?id=30571195).

ESPN. "Caitlyn Jenner Vows to 'Reshape the Landscape' in ESPYS Speech." July 16, 2015 (http://espn.go.com/espys/2015/story/_/id/13264599/caitlyn-jenner-accepts-arthur-ashe-courage-award-espys-ashe2015).

Faber, Nancy. "Bruce Jenner Seeks Olympic Gold, While Chrystie Stews." *People*, May 31, 1976.

Goldstein, Sasha, "'He Was a Stud': Bruce Jenner's Transition to Living as a Woman Shocks Longtime Racing Pal Scott Pruett." *New York Daily News*, February 18, 2015 (www.nydailynews.com/sports/more-sports/bruce-jenner-transition-shocks-racing-pal-scott-pruett-article-1.2118998).

Jenner, Bruce, and Phillip Finch. *Decathlon Challenge: Bruce Jenner's Story*. Englewood Cliffs, NJ: Prentice-Hall, 1977.

Kinon, Christina. "E! Renews 'Keeping Up with the Kardashians.'" *Daily News*, November 13, 2007 (www.nydailynews.com/entertainment/tv-movies/e-renews-keeping-kardashians-article-1.260586).

McBeen, Thomas Page. "Caitlyn Jenner, Trans Champion: 'Maybe This Is Why God Put Me On Earth.'" *Glamour*, October 29, 2015 (www.glamour.com/inspired/women-of-the -year/2015/caitlyn-jenner).

Miller, Julie. "Dressing Caitlyn Jenner: V.F.'s Jessica Diehl on Secret Shopping Runs and Classic Silhouettes." VanityFair.com, June 1, 2015 (http://www.vanityfair.com /hollywood/2015/06/caitlyn-jenner-bruce -cover-style).

Moraski, Lauren. "Caitlyn Jenner's 'I Am Cait' Gets Season 2." CBS News, October 22, 2015 (www.cbsnews.com/news/caitlyn -jenner-gets-season-2-of-i-am-cait).

Ottum, Bob. "Hey, Mister Fantasy Man…Otherwise Known as Bruce Jenner." *Sports Illustrated*, November 3, 1980. p. 78.

People magazine. "The Caitlyn Jenner Story." *People Special Edition*, 2015.

Shinn, Peggy. "How Bruce Jenner Became the 'World's Greatest Athlete.'" Team USA.org, April 30, 2015 (www.teamusa.org /News/2015/April/30/How-Bruce-Jenner -Became-The-Worlds-Greatest-Athlete).

Strohm, Emily. "I Was Terrified to Tell the Kids About My Transition." People.com, April 24,

2015 (www.people.com/article/bruce
-jenner-interview-transgender-kids
-support-brandon-brody-cassandra).

Thompson, Linda. "How Living with and Loving Bruce Jenner Changed My Life Forever." *Huffington Post*, April 4, 2015 (www
.huffingtonpost.com/linda-thompson
/bruce-jenner-linda-thompson_b_7080918
.html).

Time magazine. "A Glittering Quest for Gold." August 9, 1976, p. 60.

INDEX

ABOUT THE AUTHOR

Carla Mooney is a graduate of the University of Pennsylvania. She writes for young people, and she is the author of many books for young adults and children. She enjoys learning about the lives of the world's most fascinating people.

PHOTO CREDITS

Cover, pp. 1, 79 Kevin Winter/Getty Images; pp. 4–5 Larry Busacca/Getty Images; p. 9 © Bob Caddick/Alamy Stock Photo; p. 14 Paul Popper/Popperfoto/Getty Images; p. 19 G.N. Lowrance/Getty Images; p. 20 tichr/Shutterstock.com; p. 22 Images Press/Archive Photos/Getty Images; p. 24 Allen Steele/Getty Images; p. 27 Hulton Archive/Archive Photo/Getty Images; p. 29 James Drake/Sports Illustrated/Getty Images; p. 35 Heinz Kluetmeier/Sports Illustrated/Getty Images; pp. 37, 47, 48, 58 Ron Galella/Ron Galella Collection/Getty Images; p. 40 © AP Images; pp. 41, 61 Donaldson Collection/Michael Ochs Archives/Getty Images; p. 53 Kevin Winter/The LIFE Picture Collection/Getty Images; p. 64 Alberto E. Rodriguez/Getty Images; p. 69 Dimitrios Kambouris/E/Getty Images Entertainment/Getty Images; p. 77 Eastfjord Productions/shutterstock.com; p. 83 Mladen Antonov/AFP/Getty Images; pp. 86, 89 Kevin Mazur/WireImage/Getty Images; cover and interior pages graphic pattern L. Kramer/Shutterstock.com. Designer: Ellina Litmanovich; Photo Researcher: Carina Finn